TIME TRAVELING TO
1963

CELEBRATING A SPECIAL YEAR

TIME TRAVELING TO 1963

Author

Richard J. Thomas

Design

Gonçalo Sousa

December 2022

ISBN: 9798366458412

Surprise!

Dear reader, thank you so much for purchasing my book!

To make this book more (much more!) affordable, the images are all black & white, but I've created a special gift for you!

You can now have access, for FREE, to the PDF version of this book with the original images!

Keep in mind that some are originally black & white, but a lot of them are colored.

Go to page 99 and follow the instructions to download it.

I hope you enjoy it!

Contents

Chapter I: News & Current Events 1963

Leading Events   9

Other Major Events   13

Political Events   16

Other Notable Events   21

Chapter II: Crime & Punishment 1963   29

Chapter III: Entertainment 1963

Silver Screen   33

Top Of The Charts   42

Television   46

Chapter IV: Sports Review 1963

American Sports   51

British Sports   55

International Sports   57

Chapter V: General 1963

Pop Culture   59

Technological Advancements   63

Fashion   67

Cars of 1963   69

Popular Recreation   75

Chapter VI: Births & Deaths 1963

Births   79

Deaths   81

Chapter VII: Statistics 1963   85

Cost Of Things   88

Chapter VIII: Iconic Advertisements of 1963   91

Chapter I: News and Current Events 1963

Leading Events

March: The Beatles release debut album "Please, Please Me"

The Beatles

With the release of their debut record "Please, Please Me" in March of 1963, the Beatles unleashed a phenomenon that swept Britain, followed by the US and the entire world the following year. Unseen before or since in such magnitude, the effect of the Fab Four on women was such that after six short years of live performance, by 1966 the band decided they could no longer perform live and never toured again. The screaming drowned out the music and also made it unsafe for them to travel. It was hysteria on a mass level.

The release of this record not only proved to be popular however, it also turned music as we had known it upside down. The Beatles (along with others of their time) helped to bridge the gap between black and white music. They experimented with different recording techniques, broke

'Psychedelic Music'

away from the "standards", and blended eastern and western instruments as well as ideas. It was not merely the music which they influenced, it was an entire way of life.

They are credited with being among the first to make "psychedelic music", to make experimental drug use popular, to challenge the status quo, and to ultimately have a massive influence on what became the counterculture of the later 1960's. The Beatles changed the world with the release of Please, Please Me.

August 28th, 1963: Martin Luther King gives historical "I have a Dream" speech.

Martin Luther King Jr. at the March on Washington

In the United States on August 28th, 1963, 200,000 people marched to Washington and gathered at the Lincoln Memorial in demand of their civil rights. The marchers were fighting for their equality, jobs and freedom, and the event brought all the leading civil rights leaders of the time, including Dr. Martin Luther King Jr. His speech "I have a Dream" has gone down in American history, and the world beyond as one of the most memorable speeches of recent history. The influence of this speech was so powerful that it proved to be a turning point in the fight for civil rights and helped to initiate change in the policies of the American federal government. The passing of the Civil Rights Act of 1964, the Voting Rights Act of 1965, and the end of segregation were all direct results of the power of Dr. King's speech, not to mention the source of inspiration for the generations who have come after.

August 30th: US and Soviet Union agree on a "hotline" after Cuban Missile Crisis

After the Cuban Missile Crisis of October 1962 in which it was discovered that Russia had planted a nuclear missile on the island of Cuba, a direct line was finally formed between the

White House Kremlin "hotline"

president of the United States and his Russian counterpart in August of 1963. The necessity of this development was obvious during the missile crises when it became clear that the traditional forms of communication were far too cumbersome and slow in the event of a true emergency. At the time, encrypted messages needed to be relayed via overseas telegram, telegraph, or radioed between the two countries. In such a "hot" environment, the possibility of accident, misunderstanding or miscalculation were great.
It worked like this: the president would relay a message to the Pentagon via phone. The Pentagon would type the message into a teletype machine, encrypt it, and then feed it into a transmitter. The message would reach the Kremlin within minutes.

November 22nd: Kennedy Assassination

Friday, November 22, 1963, at 12:30pm was the day of one of America's most tragic events in its history. President John F. Kennedy was assassinated in Dallas, Texas while riding in his presidential motorcade. The President received a fatal shot, and the motorcade was immediately rushed to Parkland Memorial Hospital. The much beloved President John F. Kennedy was pronounced dead thirty minutes later.

THE ASSASSINATION OF PRESIDENT KENNEDY

LIFE Magazine November 29, 1963

Lee Harvey Oswald

Lee Harvey Oswald was charged with the murders of Kennedy and detained later that same night, though he denied shooting anyone and claimed he was being made the scapegoat for something/someone else, because he had lived in the Soviet Union.

Later the following evening, as Oswald was being transported from the basement of the Dallas police station to a more secure location, Lee Harvey Oswald himself was assassinated by a man named Jack Ruby, an owner of several strip clubs and bars in the area and who had ties to organized crime. He claimed that he was in a rage over the Oswald's assassination of Kennedy and that the rage caused him to go into a state of amnesia. He claimed to have no memory of himself shooting Oswald. Ruby died in prison four years later. The assassination of JFK has remained as one of America's most prolific conspiracy theories, however. The American public has never taken the Warren Commission's findings at face value, and in 1979 the United States

House Select Committee on Assassinations concluded that Kennedy was likely "assassinated as a result of a conspiracy," after analysis of a dictabelt audio recording taken from an open radio microphone worn on the belt of a policeman who'd been

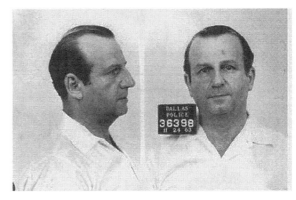

Jack Ruby

riding behind the presidential vehicle. They also concluded that there was a 95% chance that there was a fourth shot fired as well as a second gunman and that the third of the four shots fired came not from the book depository, but from a grassy knoll to the right and just ahead of the president's vehicle. The American people still do not know whether their president was assassinated by the lone gunman Lee Harvey Oswald, or whether a more sinister conspiracy was at play, with the perpetrators having never been caught.

Other Major Events

USA: Birmingham Demonstrations for Civil Rights, April 3rd

A 17-year-old Civil Rights demonstrator is attacked by a police dog in Birmingham, Alabama: this photo led to the front page of the New York Times.

In the spring of 1963 Martin Luther King staged a protest campaign in Birmingham, Alabama to undermine the city's segregation policies. The demonstrations consisted of sit-ins, boycotts, mass protests and a march to city hall. They continued through the summer, but the violence against them by the police, the Klu Klux Klan, and police dogs created widespread anger at the violence against the protests and led up to the March on Washington later in the year, JFK's civil rights bill, and the KKK attack in September.

Russia: Valentina Tereshkova – The First Woman in Space, June 16th

Valentina Tereshkova

Valentina Tereshkova became the youngest and first woman in space in the world when she flew a solo mission on the Vostok 6 and orbited the Earth 48 times. She spent nearly three days in space and still remains the only woman to have ever been on a solo space mission. She began her career as an amateur skydiver and joined the Air Force as part of the Cosmonaut Corps. The first female group of female cosmonauts was later dissolved, but Tereshkova remained as an instructor.

International: Nuclear Test-Ban Treaty, August 5th

In the decades preceding the 1963 ban on nuclear testing, the levels of TNT in the atmosphere were becoming dangerously high and outcry from the public over what this meant for health, the environment and nuclear proliferation was finally heard by governments. At the time of its origination,

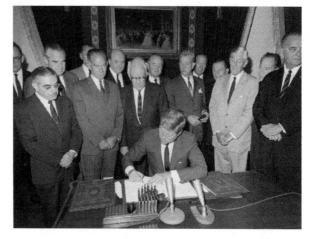

Pres. John F. Kennedy signing the Nuclear Test-Ban Treaty

only the Soviet Union, the US, and UK signed the treaty. But since then, 123 countries have come on board. Ten countries remain signed but unratified, including the United States. India, Pakistan, and North Korea have not signed it at all. The treaty coincided with falling levels of atmospheric radiation and nuclear proliferation.

USA: Implementation of the zip-code system

By the early 1960's, a more organized system of classifying addresses in cities in the US was needed. The "zone improvement plan" aka the ZIP code was implemented to help this system. The acronym was chosen not only for the accurate definition of the words that make it up, but also for the suggestion that it would make mail travel quicker and more efficient.

Mr. ZIP, the United States Post Office Department mascot

Switzerland: The Sedative Valium (chlordiazepoxide) is Developed by Roche Labs

F. Hoffmann-La Roche & Co. founded in Basel, Switzerland

In the mid 1950's, Roche labs accidentally discovered the compound chlordiazepoxide while studying a class of dyes. They found that the compound had several therapeutic effects including that of being a muscle relaxant, having hypnotic characteristics, and general quieting effects. Further studies on rats, cats and dogs all showed it to have similar properties. Once they moved onto human studies, it showed to have especially good effects on alcoholics and those suffering from dermatologic issues deriving from stress. In 1963 it was launched with a new name: Valium.

Belgium: Cassette Tape Invented by Philips

An audio cassette tape

In September of 1963 the Dutch company Philips developed the compact cassette tape. It was originally designed for dictation but improvements in fidelity soon meant that it could replace the 8-track and the reel to reel in most settings. It's small size, durability and ease of use meant that it was extremely popular with users and became the leading form of listening to music before the CD took its place in the 1990's.

Political Events

Britain: The Profumo Scandal

A major scandal in British politics in which John Profumo, the Secretary of State for War had an affair with Christine Keeler, a 19-year-old call girl. Public interest was heightened when it came to light that not only was she nineteen, and a call girl, but that she was also

John Profumo

Christine Keeler

having an affair with two other men, one of whom was a Soviet naval attaché, creating a possible major national security risk. The scandal undermined the credit of the current government and the Prime Minister Harold MacMillan resigned later that year, resulting in the conservative government's defeat to the Labor party.

US: Gideon Vs. Wainwright

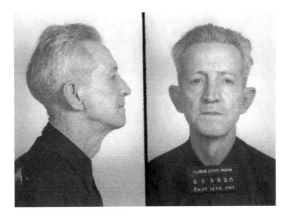

Clarence Earl Gideon mugshot

Gideon Vs. Wainwright was a landmark case decision of the US Supreme Court which determined that every defendant has the right to be represented and that an attorney shall be appointed by the court if they cannot afford one. Gideon was charged in a Florida court for a misdemeanor and during the trail he asked for the judge to appoint counsel because he could not afford one. Florida law stated that only defendants with capital offenses could be permitted counsel. The judge denied his request and he was left to defend himself in court – and lost. Several years later he appealed his case, and it was taken up by the Supreme Court, who upheld that the sixth and fourteenth Amendments guarantee a right of legal counsel in the state courts.

Vietnam: 75-year-old Buddhist Monk Sets Himself on Fire

On June 11th, 1963, a Buddhist monk, Thich Quang Duc, burned himself to death in the middle of a busy intersection in protest of the persecution of

Buddhists in South Vietnam
by the government of Ngo
Dinh Diem, a Roman
Catholic. Duc's act of self-
immolation generated such
attention world-wide that
it forced Diem to announce
reforms in his policies
towards Buddhists, but they
were never implemented, and

Thich Quang Duc

the conflict escalated when Diem's brother used the Special Forces to launch
raids on Buddhist pagodas and causing many deaths. Many monks followed
Duc's example and immolated themselves in protest. The conflict continued
until November 2, when the US backed a coup which ended with Diem's
assassination.

Vietnam: Military Coup

In November of 1963, President Ngo
Dinh Diem and the Personalist Labor
Revolutionary Party of South Vietnam were
deposed by several Army of the Republic
of Vietnam officers who disagreed with his
handling of the Buddhist crisis and the Viet
Cong threat to the regime. The Kennedy
administration had been aware of the
planning of the coup, but according to Cable
243 from the United States Department
of State to the U.S. Ambassador to South
Vietnam Henry Cabot Lodge Jr., the U.S.
policy was not to try to stop it. The coup

During ceremonies at Saigon

was led by General Duong Van Minh and began on November first, 1963. Loyalist leaders were captured after being caught off-guard and casualties were light. Diem was captured and executed the next day along with his brother and adviser Ngo Dinh Ngu.

Rebel tanks are drawn up in front of the presidential palace in Saigon Duc

Yugoslavia: President Tito President for Life

Josip Broz Tito

On April 7th, 1963, Yugoslavia created a constitution proclaiming Tito the president for life of the Socialist Federal Republic of Yugoslavia. In 1953, Tito was elected Yugoslav president and was continuously re-elected until 1963, when his term was made unlimited. Although he used the secret police to purge political opponents, most Yugoslavians enjoyed more freedoms than the inhabitants of any other communist country in Eastern Europe. Tito died in May 1980, a few days' shy of his 88th birthday.

Greece: Parliamentary Elections Held in Favor of Georgios Papandreou

On November 3rd, 1963, Parliamentary elections were held in Greece resulting in a narrow victory for the Center Union of Georgios Papandreou after three consecutive victories of Konstantinos Karamanlis and his National Radical Union after 11 years, during which time the conservative parties (Greek Rally and its successor, the National Radical Union) ruled Greece. The early elections were caused by the resignation of Karamanlis who was so incensed by King Paul I that he preferred to resign and leave the country rather than fight. It was a fierce confrontation with King Paul I and the royal family that led to the fall of the right-wing government.

Georgios Papandreou

Korea: South Korea Returns to Civilian Rule

Major-General Park Chung-hee (center) and soldiers

After the military coup in 1961, in which South Korea had been ruled the reformist military Supreme Council for National Reconstruction led by Park Chung-hee which had rendered powerless the democratically elected government of Prime Minister Chang Myon and President Yun Posun, and ended the Second Republic, South Korea returned to civilian rule once more on October 15th, 1963. The election narrowly resulted in a victory for the acting incumbent and leader, Park Chung-hee. However, there were several irregularities. General Park Chung-hee had agreed to return the power to civil politicians on April eighth 1963, but announced at the same time that he would run for the presidency of the new civilian government, after also announcing his plans to extend the military rule for another four years.

Although the election "returned South Korea to civilian rule", Park served as a dictator for nearly 18 years before he was assassinated in 1979.

Other Notable Events

President Kennedy Visits Berlin

President John F. Kennedy delivers his Berlin Speech

On June 26th, 1963, the President of the United States, John F. Kennedy made a memorable speech in Berlin. In the speech, he offered American solidarity to the citizens of West Germany. 120,000 Berliners gathered in front of the City Hall to hear the President of the United States speak. When he appeared on the stage, he was given a several minutes-long ovations, after which he told the crowd that West Berlin was a symbol of freedom for a world threatened by the Cold War. He ended the speech with the quote: "All free men, wherever they may live, are citizens of Berlin, and therefore, as a free man, I take pride in the words, 'Ich bin ein Berliner'" ("I am a Berliner"). The speech was seen as a turning point in the Cold War and was a major morale booster for West Germans, who were worried about the Berlin Wall, recently built. The

120,000 Berliners gathered

speech also gave a strong message to the Soviet Union and had the effect of putting down Moscow's desire of driving the Allies out of West Berlin. It was two months later that President Kennedy negotiated the first nuclear test ban treaty with the Soviet Union, which was seen as a first step towards ending the Cold War.

USA: Alcatraz Closes

Alcatraz prison island

The notorious maximum-security island in the San Francisco Bay closed down on March 21st, 1963, after having begun as a fort in the US civil war, then becoming a military prison, and finally ending as a maximum-security federal penitentiary. It was due to the high cost of daily maintenance and repairs that the island was finally abandoned by the federal government. During it's time as a prison, it held such notorious criminals as Al Capone, Robert Stroud and James Bulger and also boasted some of the most cutting-edge technology of the time, including the use of the first metal detectors. It was notoriously brutal for the unfortunate inmates that found themselves there. A complete silence policy was enforced nearly all day. Because of the high security and its

Inside the prison

location in the middle of the cold, shark infested waters with strong currents surrounding the island, it was considered escape proof. Over the years, there had been 36 attempts, all of which ended in being shot, drowning, or re-captured. However, just the year before its closing three inmates attempted an escape and to this day nobody knows if they succeeded. A letter was sent to the FBI in 2018 claiming to be one of the three escapees, but investigations failed to prove the claim.

USA: James Meredith becomes the first African American to graduate from the University of Mississippi

James Meredith, accompanied by federal officials, enrolls at the University of Mississippi

James Howard Meredith is an American civil rights activist, writer, political adviser, and Air Force veteran. In 1962 he became the first African-American student admitted to the racially segregated University of Mississippi and in 1963 he became the first to graduate from its walls. He decided to embark on this bold journey after listening to the inspiring inaugural address by John F. Kennedy and with the intention of putting pressure on the federal government to make decisive changes for the civil rights of the African Americans and to end segregation.

Kenya: Kenya gains independence from Britain

Kenya gained its independence from British Colonial Rule on December 12th, 1963, after a decade of strife following the Mau Mau uprising in 1952 which had badly shaken the British colony. During the uprising, the British

Kenya gained independence from Britain

spent £55 million on its suppression, carried out massacres of civilians and forced many hundreds of thousands of Kenyans into concentration camps. After the uprising, they imprisoned and executed many of the leader rebels. However, it was clear that England no longer had the money or the power to sustain its colony and, in the years, preceding the independence, the British made concessions for the Kenyan citizens. They were allowed to own land, grow coffee, and were allowed to be elected to the Legislative Council beginning in 1967. Plans were drawn up to give Kenya its independence and a Kenyan government was formed, with Jomo Kenyatta, a previously imprisoned rebel leader, to be the first Prime Minister of Kenya. Following independence, Kenyatta implemented a one-party rule and ruled over a corrupt and autocratic government until his death in 1978. His son took over as Prime Minister in 2013, and still is today in 2022.

USA: Nuclear-powered attack submarine USS Thresher sinks in the Atlantic Ocean

On the morning of April 10th, 1963, the USS Skylark received communication that the USS Thresher was experiencing minor problems. Both vessels had been participating in routine

USS Thresher

drills off the coast of New England. The Thresher was the very first of a new class of submarine designed to be quieter and with the capability of diving deeper than any other before. Only five short minutes between Thresher's first attempt at communication, radar images showed the submarine breaking into pieces as it hit the bottom of the ocean floor. All on board were killed. Later investigation of the USS Thresher revealed that a leak in a silver-brazed joint in the engine room had caused a short circuit in critical electrical systems. Though a tragedy, because of the sinking of the Thresher, improvements in the design and quality control of submarines were greatly improved and prove to be much safer today as a result.

USA: The Birmingham Riot of May 1963

The riots of May 1963 in Birmingham, Alabama were triggered by the bombings of black-owned business, the parsonage of Rev. A.D. King, Martin Luther King's brother which ended in the murder of three adolescent

Firemen turn fire hoses on demonstrators

girls. It was believed that the bombings were carried out by the local KKK in coordination with the Birmingham police. What began as a non-violent protest directed by Doctor King, soon became a violent riot, as the black community decided that non-violence was not working. The federal government intervened for the very first time in a situation like this when the blatantly racist Alabama governor George Wallace brought in federal troops to squash the riot.

USA: First US lottery, New Hampshire

N.H. Governor John King buys the first N.H. Sweepstakes ticket

In 1963 the New Hampshire Sweepstakes was approved and formed by the New Hampshire General Court State Legislature, at the behest of Representative Larry Pickett, of Keene, NH, who had been trying to get the idea approved for a decade. On March 10th, a special election was held which allowed residents of New Hampshire to vote for or against the sale of Sweepstakes tickets. Twelve towns out of 224 (New London, New Hampton, Dummer, Lyman, Monroe, Piermont, Hollis, Sharon, Durham and Madbury) each voted against the measure. Sweepstakes tickets went on sale two days later, on March 12th, 1964. At first, the New Hampshire Sweepstakes was conducted by horse races at Salem's Rockingham Park, with the winning numbers based on the races, rather than simply drawing numbers from a barrel or using ping pong balls. This was done in order to avoid violating US anti-lottery statutes. Tickets were usually sold in the state's liquor stores. The New Hampshire Lottery offered online lottery tickets for the first time in September of 2018.

Australia and New Zealand: Queen Elizabeth and Prince Philip Return

For the first time since the hugely popular royal tour of 1953-54, the Royals returned to New Zealand followed by Australia. During the trip to New Zealand, the Queen announced the Royal Victorian Order, to mark the visit. She and the Duke of Edenborough also attended celebrations at Waitangi. The honors were announced on February 11th and 18th, 1963, before moving on to Australia where they arrived for the Jubilee Year of the naming

Queen Elizabeth II making her Christmas broadcast to the people of the Commonwealth

of the capital city Canberra. The visit to Australia consisted of a 9,000-mile journey on the continent. However, the journey was done via the Royal Yacht Britannia. Having spent 8 weeks travelling to every part of Australia in 1954, the Queen had decided that the use of the Britannia as a permanent base would be a more comfortable journey, allowing her to entertain aboard ship and rest between each port as she travelled the 9,000 miles around Australia's coastline.

The Queen delivered a rousing rooftop speech for the opening of the Royal Children's Hospital, where she said "A monument to Victoria's humanity and public spirit" thus, making official the opening of the hospital. Queen Elizabeth II and Prince Philip would return to Melbourne in 2011 to be present for the current hospital which was built next door to the first Parkville hospital.

One funny story that purportedly occurred during the trip was when the Queen threw shoes and a racket at Prince Philip during a row. According to the book Prince Philip Revealed, a camera operator for a film crew which was trailing the couple during a rare weekend off during

Queen Elizabeth II, Prince Philip and Princess Anne with Te Atairangikaahu, the Maori queen, in New Zealand

the tour happened to witness Philip charging out of the couple's chalet, "followed by a flying pair of tennis shoes and a racket and a very angry Queen shouting for him to come back. Then the indignant Queen grabbed hold of her husband and dragged him back inside."

Chapter II: Crime and Punishment 1963

Australia: Serial killer Eric Edgar Cooke caught

Eric Edgar Cooke

On September 1st, 1963, Eric Edgar Cooke was caught and captured after trying to retrieve a rifle which he had hid in a bush. The rifle had been found and reported to the police who inspected it and determined that it had been used in a murder the previous month. Officers set up a decoy rifle, connected it with fishing line and set up a "hide" in case the perpetrator returned. When he did, he was arrested and finally admitted to several killings which up to that point the police had considered unconnected due to there being no obvious connection between victims. He also killed with many different weapons and used several different styles of rifles, stabbed his victims with scissors, ax, knives, strangled with rope, and hit with his car. Sometimes he robbed the homes of victims, other times he just murdered them. He would sometimes hang around afterwards and enjoy a beverage and at least once, committed necrophilia. He was sentenced to execution by hanging and died on October 26th, 1964. His refused to appeal, stating that he deserved his sentence.

Sicily: The Ciaculli Massacre and the First Mafia War

On the 30th of June 1963 a car bomb went off outside of Palermo, in Ciaculli, Sicily, killing 7 police and military officers who'd been sent to diffuse it after receiving an anonymous phone call. The bomb was meant for Salvatore Greco, head of the Sicilian Mafia commission. Known ever after as the Ciaculli Massacre, the event was the culmination of a war between mafia families,

Funeral for the seven police and military officers

but public outrage soon turned it into a war against the mafia. The First Mafia war had begun in 1962, but after the Ciaculli Massacre the state made a concerted effort against the mafia for the first time and as a result many mafias fled to other parts of the world. In a period of ten weeks, 1,200 mafias were arrested, many of whom were kept off the streets for as long as five or six years and the Sicilian Mafia Commission was dissolved. Those who managed to escape left Italy for United States, Canada, Argentina, Brazil, and Venezuela where they managed to set up other mafia organizations. The Italian government was so outraged by the event; they were galvanized to implement a law for the Anti-Mafia Commission. The commission met for the first time on July 6th, 1963.

Britain: The Great Train Robbery

The Great Train Robbery took place on the West Coast Main Line of the Royal Mail train on August 8th, 1963, at the Bridego Railway Bridge, near Mentmore in Buchinghamshire, England. The heist had been perfectly planned with information from the inside and was executed equally well with the perpetrators escaping with £2.6 million. The gang of 15 who committed the robbery, led by Bruce Reynolds, and one of whom was a retired train driver, did so by tampering with the lineside signals and bringing the train to a stop. Once the train was stopped, they attacked, and the heist was carried out without the use of a single firearm. The bulk of the money was never recovered, however most of the gang was eventually caught when police discovered their hangout not long after the train heist.

Crime Scene Photograph of the Great Train Robbery of 1963

USA: 16th Street Baptist Church Bombing

The 16th Street Baptist church was a very popular establishment with the black community of Birmingham, particularly with the leaders of the civil rights movement and including Dr. Martin Luther King Jr. On the morning of Sunday, September 15th, 1963, at 10:22am when the church had 200 parishioners inside in pre-service Sunday school, a bomb went off. Twenty parishioners were injured in the attack and four young girls were killed, found in the rubble of the basement restroom. The attack took place 11 days after the federal court order mandated that schools be desegregated. Most of the whites in Birmingham were adamantly against desegregation and the town was home to one of the strongest and most violent contingents of Ku Klux Klan in the South. The

The four girls killed in the bombing

city's police commissioner Eugene "Bull" Connor was notoriously racist, demonstrating his willingness to use brutality against blacks, activists, and union members. Precisely for its reputation as a center for white supremacists did Dr. King choose Birmingham as the central focus of his cause. So many bombs had gone off in the city in the early '60's that by 1963 it had earned the nickname "Bombingam".

USA: Jack Ruby murders Lee Harvey Oswald

Detective James R. Leavelle, glowered as Jack Ruby shot Lee Harvey Oswald

On the evening of November 24th, Jack Ruby, the owner of several strip clubs and bars in the city of Dallas, Texas, shot Lee Harvey Oswald, the man accused of assassinating the president of the United States, John F. Kennedy two days prior. Ruby claimed that his outrage at Oswald for killing Kennedy caused him to suffer psychomotor epilepsy and murder Oswald in a state of unconsciousness. Ruby was sentenced to die, but the decision was later reversed stating that it was impossible for Ruby to have received a fair trial in Dallas at the time of the decision. He died in 1969 in prison, of lung cancer. Jack Ruby looms large in the conspiracies surrounding the Kennedy assassination with theorists claiming that he killed Oswald in order to keep him from revealing a larger conspiracy against the president.

Chapter III: Entertainment 1963

Silver Screen

Cleopatra

Cleopatra

The top grossing film of 1963 was "Cleopatra" starring Elizabeth Taylor, Richard Burton, Rex Harrison, Roddy McDowall, and Martin Landau, bringing in a staggering $71 million at the box office worldwide ($57 million were from the domestic box office) . At $44 million it was the most expensive film ever made at that point. So much so, that despite being the highest grossing film of the year, it made little profit in the end. The film made headlines not only for the cost of production, but also because of the extra-marital affair between Taylor and Richard Burton during the filming of the movie which scandalized the public.

The movie is a saga, and epic, running a full three hours and fifty-three minutes. Directed by Joseph L. Mankiewicz, the script underwent numerous revisions, but when it finally debuted in New York June 12th, 1963, it received warm praise from the critics.

Remaining Top 3 Films

Released on February 20th, "How the West Was Won" came in second in 1963 at the box office, pulling in $21 million the weekend it was released and grossed $46.5 million, while the budget for the making of the film was

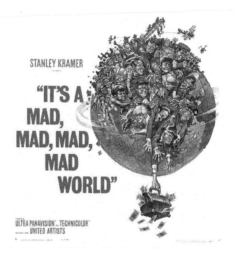

the biggest entertainment ever to rock the screen with laughter!

How the West Was Won

It's a Mad, Mad, Mad, Mad World

a mere $15 million. This western epic was directed by Henry Hathaway, narrated by Spencer Tracy and stars an ensemble cast including John Wayne, Henry Fonda, and James Stewart. "It's a Mad, Mad, Mad, Mad World" came in third for the year, a comedy starring Spencer Tracy about a group of strangers trying to steal $350,000, and "Tom Jones" came in fourth, a British comedy starring Albert Finney based on the 1749 novel 'The History of Tom Jones'. They brought in $46,3 million and $37,6 million respectively.

Tom Jones

Other Top Ten Films

Other top films of the year were "Irma La Douce", the story about a French police officer who falls in love with a prostitute, starring Jack Lemon and Shirley MacLaine and directed by Billy Wilder. The romantic comedy brought in $25,246,588

Irma La Douce

Son of Flubber

at the box office on a budget of $5 million; "Son of Flubber", a science fiction comedy and sequel to the 1961 "The Absent-Minded Professor" staring Fred MacMurray and directed by Robert Stevenson was a success as well with its plot about a scientist who discovers a high-bouncing substance called "flubber" and brought in $22,129,412; "Charade", a blend of romance-suspense-thriller and comedy starring Audrey Hepburn and Cary Grant brought in $13,474,929 on a $3 million budget. 'Charade' was praised for the direction and chemistry between Hepburn and Grant and featured the popular song "Charade" by Henry Mancini; "Bye, Bye Birdie", a musical, came in at $13,129,412 at the box office. It was Dick Van Dyke's film debut and based on the 1960

Charade

Bye, Bye Birdie

Move Over, Darling   The Great Escape   Come Blow Your Horn

musical of the same name, directed by George Sydney. The musical was based on Elvis Presley's draft into the United States Army in 1957; "Come Blow Your Horn" staring Frank Sinatra, was directed by Bud Yorkin, and was nominated for an academy award; the love-triangle/comedy "Move Over, Darling" starring Doris Day, James Garner, and Polly Bergen was a hit and tied with "Come Blow Your Horn" bringing in $12,705,882 at the box office; and finally, "The Great Escape", a film based on the non-fiction book written by Paul Brickhill in 1950, brought $11,744,471 in at the box office. The war epic starred Steve McQueen, James Garner, and Richard Attenborough and won McQueen the Best Actor award at the Moscow International Film Festival. It was also notable for the motorcycle and jump scene, which is considered one of the best stunts ever done.

🎬 Box Office Figures 1963

Top 1963 Movies at The Domestic Box Office

Rank	Title	Total Gross	Open Wknd. Gross
1	Cleopatra	57,000,000	26 million

Rank	Title	Total Gross	Open Wknd. Gross
2	How the West Was Won	46,500,000	21 million
3	It's a Mad, Mad, Mad, Mad World	46,300,000	20.8 million
4	Tom Jones	37,600,000	17 million
5	Irma La Douce	25,246,588	12 million
6	Son of Flubber	22,129,412	10 million
7	Charade	13,474,588	$35,400,000
8	Bye, Bye Birdie	13,129,412	$32,056,467
9	Come Blow Your Horn / Move Over Darling	12,705,882	$30,333,743
10	The Great Escape	11,744,471	$27,274,150

Other Film Releases

A number of other important films were released in 1963 that didn't necessarily gain acclaim at the time, but over the decades have become iconic to the period. Although released in December of 1962, "To Kill a Mockingbird" hit number one in the charts on March 13th, 1963, and has gone down in history as one of the 1960's most poignant films. In addition, Alfred Hitchcock's "The Birds", was released on March 28th.

To Kill a Mockingbird

The Birds

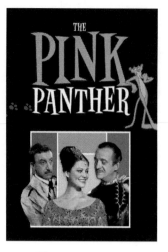

Lord of the Flies   The Pink Panther   Dr. No

"The Birds", one of the spookiest horror films of its time was also controversial after its release, when the actress Tippi Hedren later stated that she had refused advances by Hitchcock during the making of the film and that afterwards, several strange things happened on the set that she suspected were purposeful acts of vengeance on his part. "The Lord of the Flies" has also gone down as one of the most important films of its time. Based on the novel by William Golding's 1954 novel of the same name, the British drama stars Peter Brook and was directed by Peter Aubrey. "The Pink Panther" cannot be forgotten in the list of classic films released in 1963. And last but certainly not least, the very first James Bond, "Dr. No", was released on May 8th, starring Sean Connery. While none of these made the top of the charts or won awards that year, they have each surpassed the winners of the day as going down in history for being "classic" 1963 films.

21st Golden Globe Awards – Wednesday, March 11th, The Hilton, Beverly Hills, Ca.

 Winners

Best Picture Drama (Film)
The Cardinal

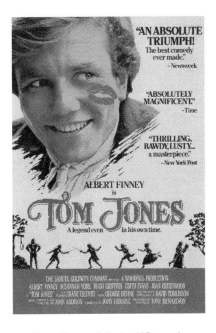

Best Picture Musical/Comedy
Tom Jones

Best Actress Motion Picture
Drama – Leslie Caron

Best Actor Motion Picture
Drama – Sidney Poitier

Best Actress Motion Picture
Musical/Comedy
Shirley MacLaine

Best Actor Motion Picture
Musical/Comedy
Alberto Sordi

Best Supporting Actress
Motion Picture
Margaret Rutherford

Best Supporting Actor Motion
Picture – John Huston

Best Director Motion
Picture – Elia Kazan

British Academy of Film and Television Arts Awards

🏆 Winners

- 🏅 Best Film – Tom Jones
- 🏅 Best British Film – Tom Jones
- 🏅 Best British Screenplay – Tom Jones

Best British Actor
Dirk Bogarde

Best British Actress
Rachel Roberts

Best Animated Film
The Critic

Best Foreign Actress – Patricia Neal

Best Foreign Actor – Marcello Mastroianni

The 37th Academy Awards – Monday, April 13th, Santa Monica Civic Auditorium, Santa Monica, CA.

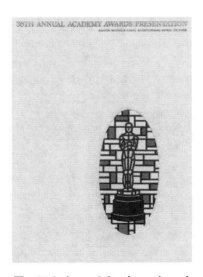

The 36th Annual Academy Awards

🏆 Winners

- Best Picture – Tom Jones
- Best Director – Tony Richardson – Tom Jones
- Best Actor – Sidney Poitier – Lilies of the Field
- Best Actress – Patricia Neal – Hud
- Best Supporting Actor – Melvyn Douglas – Hud
- Best Supporting Actress – Margaret Rutherford – The V.I.P.'s
- Best Music – John Addison – Tom Jones
- Best Song – Call Me Irresponsible – Papa's Delicate Condition
- Best Art Direction – Cleopatra
- Best Cinematography (color) – Cleopatra
- Best Costume – Cleopatra
- Best Visual Effects – Cleopatra

Top Of The Charts

Beatlemania, the advent of surf music, the folk revival, funk, blues, Motown, were all making a huge splash in the music world, changing how we listen and make music forever in the early 1960's. In fact, even today, music is considered one of the most important aspects of the 1960's. Music became the preferred form of entertainment, particularly with the youth and outstripped the television and film industries in popularity for the first time. While the music of the early 1960's seems mild compared to the music of 2022, at the time it was revolutionary. It is difficult to gather accurate information regarding the exact statistics regarding sales figures, but finding the top ten most popular on the charts is not as difficult.

The website tsort.info is a good source for locating the top of the charts.

Best Album: James Brown Live At the Apollo

The top-rated album of the year was "James Brown's Live at the Apollo".
The record was recorded live and provided
the basis for the viability of releasing live
records for the recording industry. Known
as the Godfather of Soul, James Brown
helped transform the music sung in black
churches all over the US (gospel), to the soul
wrenching, emotional, gyrating performance
of soul and funk music as we know it today. It
sold over a million copies and spent sixty-six
weeks at the top of the charts.

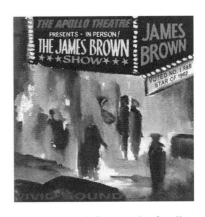

James Brown's Live at the Apollo

The Freewheelin' Bob Dylan

Please, Please Me

Best Albums and Singles

Bob Dylan's "The Freewheelin' Bob Dylan" proved to be a much more
important record than anyone could have guessed when it made its debut
in 1963. The record touched on the mood of the nation and helped to give
the youth a dialogue for how they felt about the social issues of the time.
The Beatles and the advent of Beatlemania changed the world of music, the
world over with the release of "Please, Please Me". Peter, Paul and Mary did

very well in 1963 as well, with their two records "Peter, Paul and Mary" and "Moving", and the trio helped to propel music into a more thoughtful social conscience awareness with the likes of Bob Dylan and Joan Baez, another folk singer and social activist of the 1960's.

Peter, Paul and Mary

Moving – Album by Peter, Paul, and Mary

Top Albums Of 1963 (tsort.info):

♆ Winners

1. James Brown – Live at the Apollo
2. Bob Dylan – The Freewheeling Bob Dylan
3. The Beatles – With the Beatles
4. Peter, Paul, and Mary – Peter, Paul and Mary
5. Peter, Paul, and Mary – In the Wind
6. Barbara Streisand – The Barbra Streisand Album
7. Stan Getz and Charlie Byrd – Jazz Samba
8. The Beatles – Please, Please Me
9. Peter, Paul, and Mary – Moving
10. The Singing Nun (Soeur Sourire) – The Singing Nun

Top Singles Of 1963 (tsort.info):

🏆 Winners

1. Trini Lopez – If I Had a Hammer

2. Elvis Presley – Devil in Disguise

3. Paul & Paula – Hey Paula

4. The Ronette's – Be My Baby

5. The Kingsmen – Louie Louie

6. The Fireballs – Sugar Shack

7. Kyu Sakamoto – Sukiyaki

8. Little Peggy March – I Will Follow Him

9. Singing Nun (Soeur Sourire) – Dominique

10. Ned Miller – From a Jack to a King

6th Grammy Awards, May 12th, 1964 (honoring winners of 1963) – Chicago, Las Angeles, New York

Henry Mancini (left)

🏆 Winners (Wikipedia)

- Record of The Year – Henry Mancini – Days of Wine and Roses
- Album of The Year – Barbara Streisand – The Barbara Streisand Album
- Song of The Year – Henry Mancini and Johnny Mercer – Days of Wine and Roses Best
- New Artist – Ward Swingle – The Swingle Sisters
- Best Album of Original Score Music – John Addison – Tom
- Producer of The Year (Non-Classical) – James Malloy – Charade

The Brit Awards were not yet in existence in 1963.

Television

Television in the early 60's compared to today is very different. The humor campy, the romance scenes limited, and although most families had a television by the 1960's, it was usually limited to one per household. It was also very commonly still black and white, and there were a limited number of networks. In the US the three networks were ABC, CBS, and NBC. In the UK there were merely two, the BBC and ITV.

ABC logo

CBS logo

NBC logo

BBC logo

ITV logo

The Beverly Hillbillies

The Beatles at the "Royal Variety Performance"

The number one rated show in the US was CBS's "The Beverly Hillbillies" and in the UK ITV's "The Royal Variety Performance" was number one of the year.

📺 Television Ratings 1962/63 (classic-tv.com)

Rank	Show	Audience
1	The Beverly Hillbillies	20,175,600
2	Candid Camera	15,643,300
3	The Red Skeleton Show	15,643,300
4	Bonanza	14,984,400
5	The Lucy Show	14,989,400
6	The Andy Griffith Show	14,939,100
7	Ben Casey	14,436,100
8	The Danny Thomas Show	14,236,100
9	The Dick Van Dyke Show	13,631,300
10	Gunsmoke	13,581,100

21st Golden Globe Awards – Wednesday, March 11th, The Hilton, Beverly Hills, Ca.

🏆 **Award Winners**

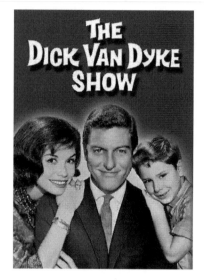

Best Drama Series
The Richard Boone Show

Best Musical/Comedy Series
The Dick Van Dyke Show

Best Series Variety
The Danny Kaye Show

Best Actor Television
Mickey Rooney – Micky

Best Actress Television –
Inger Stevens – The Farmers
Daughter

British Academy Of Film And Television Arts Awards (Wikipedia)

Best Actor
Harry H. Corbett

Best Actress (Television)
Brenda Bruce

Best Television Drama
David Rose, Charles Jarrott

Factual
Richard Cawston (on the left)

Light Entertainment
(production) – Duncan Wood

Light Entertainment
(performance) –
Michael Bentine

Desmond Davis Awards for Services to Television
Cecil McGivern

15th Primetime Emmy Awards – May 26th, Hollywood Palladium, Las Angeles, Ca.

Carol Burnett poses with her Emmy award
at the 15th Primetime Emmy Awards

🏆 Winners

- Outstanding Comedy Series – The Dick Van Dyke Show

- Outstanding Drama Series – The Defenders Outstanding Variety Show – The Andy Williams Show

- Outstanding Program in the Field of Panel, Quiz or Audience Participation – The General Electric Collage Bowl

- Outstanding Performance in a Variety or Musical Program or Series

- Outstanding Documentary Series – The Tunnel

- Best Actor – EG Marshall – The Defenders

- Best Actress – Shirley Booth – Hazel

- Best Supporting Actor – Don Knotts – The Andy Griffith Show

- Best Supporting Actress – Glenda Farrell – Ben Casey

Chapter IV: Sports Review 1963

American Sports

December 29th – 31st: Annual National Football League Championship (Wrigley Field)

1963 NFL Championship Game kicked off between the Chicago Bears and New York Giants

In 1963 the NFL had a total of 98 games in the season compared to today's 272-game season, and was the final season of the 37-man roster which was expanded to 40 the following year and in 1963 there were only 22 NFL teams compared with today's 32.

The 1963 NFL Championship Game was played between the New York Giants (Eastern Conference 11-3-0) and the Chicago Bears (Western Conference 11-1-2). This was the fifth and last NFL game played at Wrigley Field, the first being in 1933. The Yankees were in their third consecutive championship game and fifth of the previous six season and the Bears were in their first since 1956 with the Giants. The Bears beat the Yankees 14/10 with Larry Morris (Linebacker) the MVP.

April 14th-24th: National Basketball Association Finals

The 1963 NBA World Championship Series was the conclusion of the 1963 playoffs season and was played in a best of seven series of matches between the Las Angeles Lakers (Western Division) and the Boston Celtics (Eastern Division). It was the Celtics' seventh consecutive championship game and they beat the Lakers 4-2. The official score was:

NBA Champion, Boston Celtics

04/14 BC 117-114 LAL, 04/16 BC 113-106 LAL, 04/17 LAL 119-99 BC, 04/19 LAL 105-108 BC, 04/21 BC 119-126 LAL, 04/24 LAL 109-112 BC

Sam Jones was the highest scoring player for the Boston Celtics in the 1963 championship and Elgin Bayer for the LA Lakers.

Boston's Sam Jones, left, drives past the Lakers' Jerry West (44) and Darrall Imhoff, center, during a playoff game

April 9th-18th: National Hockey League Stanley Cup Finals – Toronto: Maple Leaf Gardens (1,2,5) and Detroit: Olympia (3,4)

The 1963 Stanley Cup Finals were the culmination of a 5-game series with the contesting teams being the Toronto Maple Leafs and the Detroit Red Wings. The Maple Leafs Won the best of seven series four games to one, and their second consecutive NHL championship. The official scores were:

04/9 DRW 2-4 TML,
04/11 DRW 2-4 TML,
04/14 TML 2-3 DRW,
04/16 TML 4-2 DRW,
04/18 DRW 1-3 TML

Dick Duff scored twice in the first 68 seconds of game one on Terry Sawchuk of Detroit,

Toronto Maple Leafs – Stanley Cup Champions

the fastest two goals to start a game in Stanley Cup history. In the second period, the Leafs would endure a letdown but would take the lead in the series, winning 4-2. The series-winning goal went to Eddie Shack (13:28, third, G6) who later admitted that the goal had been a stroke of luck as it had been unintentional. Afterwards, Dave Keon scored another goal, clinching their win.

August 28th-September 8th: U.S. Tennis Open

The 83rd US Open was held in Forest Hills, Queens, New York. Rafael Osuna (Mexico) defeated Frank Froehling (US) 7–5, 6–4, 6–2 in the final to win the men's singles tennis title. Maria Bueno of Brazil (fourth seeded) defeated Margaret Smith of Australia (first seeded) 7-5, 6-4.

Maria Bueno at a quarter final

Maria Bueno went on to become the most successful women's tennis player in all of South America in history and was known for her graceful style of play. She would later become the t first woman to win a calendar-year Grand Slam in doubles.

53

October 2-6th: Major League Baseball World Series

The 1963 World Series was held at both the Yankee and Dodger Stadiums, against the Yankees and the Dodgers. The Dodgers defeated the Yankees sweeping them in just four games and capturing their second title in five years and their third in franchise history.

1963 Los Angeles Dodgers

The Dodgers dominated in pitchers such that at no point in the four games were the Yankees ever ahead and the Yankees were held to a .171 team batting average, their lowest ever for post-season. It was the first time the Yankees were ever swept in four straights in the World Series. This was the only World Series (out of five) won by the Dodgers in the Dodgers Stadium and was also the first time any major professional sport had been played for a championship between New York City and Las Angeles. The official scores were:

10/2 LAD 5-2 NYY, 10/3 LAD 4-1 NYY, 10/5 NNY 0-1 LAD, 10/6 NYY 1-2 LAD

British Sports

January 12th - March 23rd:
34th Rugby Union Five Nations

The 34th Five Nations rugby 9-game
tournament was played between
England, France, Ireland, Scotland and Wales.
England won the Championship with their
17th title. The results for England were:
*01/19 Wales 6-13 England, 02/02 England
6-5 France, 02/23 Ireland 0-0 England, 03/16
England 10-8 Scotland*

Wales' Brian Price rises above
England's John Owen during
their clash in Cardiff

March 28th: Annual Oxford/Cambridge Boat Race

Sketch illustration of the men's boat race

The 109th Boat Race took
place on 23 March 1963 on
the river Thames as has been
since its conception in 1829.
Oxford won the race in 1963
by a margin of five lengths.
It was umpired by Gerald
Ellison, the Bishop of
Chester.

May 2nd: English League Cup

The 1963–64 season was the 84th season of competitive football in England,
from August 1963 to May 1964, but only the 4th season as the new English
League Cup. The competition ran through September 4th, 1963, to the
double-legged final on the 15th and 22nd of April 1964. Leicester won 4-3

on aggregate. Results of the final were:

04/15 Stoke City 1-1 Leicester City, 04/22 Leicester City 3-2 Stoke City

92 teams played in the final with the defending champions being Birmingham City. 383 goals were scored (3.68 per match).

Birmingham City League Cup winners from 1963

June 24th-July 8th: 77th Wimbledon

Margaret Smith of Australia holds up the trophy after winning the women's singles

The 77th Wimbledon Championship took place at the All England Lawn and Croquet All England Lawn Tennis and Croquet in Wimbledon, London, and was also the third Grand Slam tennis event of the year. Originally the final day was set for July 6th, but wet and rainy weather conditions meant that the final Saturday was cancelled for the women's singles, men's and women's doubles, and mixed doubles and had to be rescheduled for the following Monday, July 8th. The season was also notable for it being the first season that introduced the requirement of the predominance of white to be worn by the players. The winners of the Championship were:

Men's Singles – Chuck McKinley (US)

Women's Singles – Margaret Smith (AUS)

Men's Doubles – Rafael Osuna/Antonio Palafox (MEX)

Women's Doubles – Maria Bueno (BRAZIL)/Darlene Hard (US)

Mixed Doubles – Margaret Smith/Ken Fletcher (AUS)

Boys Singles – Nicholas Kalogeropoulos (GR)

Girls Singles – Monique Salfati (FR)

International Sports

May 26th-December 28th: Formula 1 Motor Racing

Jim Clark Lotus 49 Ford

The 1963 Formula One racing season consisted of 10 races and featured the 14th FIA World Championship of Drivers, the sixth International Cup for F1 Manufacturers, and several non-championships Formula One races. The circuit began at the Monaco Grand Prix and finished at the South African Grand Prix. Jim Cark (England) was the champion (7-2) and took home his first will in a revised Ferrari with a time of 1:34.3. His record was not beaten until 1988, but he went on to be placed at the top of a list of best-ever Formula One drivers. Graham Hill (England) was the runner up with a time of 1:35.0.

March 17th- December 28th: 52nd Davis Cup Final Adelaide, Australia

The Davis Cup, the most important of the men's national teams of tennis consisted of 32 teams in the Europe Zone, 9 teams in the Eastern Zone,

Stan Smith (USA) in Davis Cup Final

and 7 in the America zone. It is notable for the fact that Rhodesia joined the Cup for the first time. The US beat Venezuela in the America Zone final match, India defeated Japan in the Eastern Zone final, and Great Britain defeated Sweden in the Europe Zone. The US defeated Great Britain in the semifinal, and then defeated India in the final and emerged as the champions of the year, beating Australia in the final round, and ending it's 4-year title run.

May 22nd – European Cup Final, Wembley Stadium

The 1963 European Cup Final was a football match featuring Milan vs. Benfica. Milan won the match for the first time, 2–1. Benfica made their third consecutive appearance in the final, having won both the 1961 and 1962 finals. The match marked the very first win for a European Cup title for Italy and was also the first time that a Spanish team was absent from a European Cup Final.

The AC. Milan team

Chapter V: General

Pop Culture

The '60's were a thriving time in the areas of art, music, social change, and culture. As always, it is the artists that reflect the underbelly of any given period of time and 1963 was no exception. This was true with the artists of the time in the areas of fine art, preforming art, music, writing, and even architectural and automotive design.

In the early 1960's, art was thriving in new and exciting areas. Pop art became a dominant feature of the 60's – the famous Campbells soup cans silkscreens by Andy Warhol being perhaps the most famous of the time. Performance art too became very popular. Artists of all genres were pushing boundaries and challenging the status quo.

Andy Warhol

Known as the King of Pop Art, Andy Warhol rented his first studio, an old firehouse at 159 East 87th Street. It was here that he not only produced the silkscreen images of Campbells soup that became an instant hit and made him famous, but it was also here at this studio, where he created his Elvis series and his Elizabeth Taylor portraits.

Later that year, Warhol relocated a new studio to East 47th Street, which would become the infamous studio known as "The Factory".

Andy Warhol

Warhol inside "The Factory"

"The Factory" became iconic all in itself and was a popular gathering spot for a wide range of artists, writers, musicians, and underground celebrities. It even had its own band, The Velvet Underground.

The Mona Lisa

In February 1963, the government of the French Republic made a loan of "The Mona Lisa" directly to the President of the United States and the American People. It was accompanied on its journey overseas by the French Minister of Cultural Affairs, André Malraux and all of the affairs regarding arrangements and safety were done by the white house and was guarded at all times by the United Sates Marines. The painting was so popular that the museum extended its hours of operation into the evening and visitors waited up to two hours in line to view "The Mona Lisa".

Da Vinci's Mona Lisa

Carolee Schneemann

Performance art became extremely popular in the early sixties. Artists such as Carolee Schneemann excelled in pushing boundaries. In 1963 Schneemann rented an old, abandoned fur manufacturing workshop and set up a studio where she would produce art, live, and even do performance-based pieces. In

1963 she performed a piece entitled "Eye Body: 36 Transformative Actions" in which she performed naked, her body painted to reinforce the connection between the art materials and the human body. The piece also included feathers, mirror chards, snakes, as well as other materials. Her intention was for her body to become integral with the piece – becoming both the object and subject.

Eye Body: 36 Transformative Actions

Gloria Steinem

The social movements that swept the US were not limited to the civil rights movement. Women's rights and women's activism was another area of social change that was extremely active in the early '60's. Gloria Steinem was among the leading activists of the era and helped to inform the American public about the need for reform on the subject. In 1963 she made headlines when she released her two-part article about her experience working undercover at the New York Playboy Club, "A Bunny's Tale". Her experience helped to shine a light on the exploitation of women in the workplace and had the direct effect of banning the "physical examinations" as part of the application process for a playboy bunny. For many years after she regretted the article, it being the thing that her admirers and foes alike

Gloria Steinem

would forever associate with her, but in her book entitled Outrageous Acts and Everyday Rebellions she is quoted as saying "My expose of working in a Playboy Club has outlived all the Playboy Clubs, both here and abroad."

Julia Child

Publicity portrait of Julia Child in her kitchen

Julia Child's The French Chef debuted on WGBH TV in 1963 for the first time, introducing America to French cuisine and cooking. Her voice, her hearty handling of a knife, and love of wine and butter soon became a staple in the American home and was WGBH's longest serving program. The show is also notable for being the first series on WGBH where captions were introduced for the deaf and hearing impaired.

Books released in 1963

- Planet of the Apes – Pierre Boulle
- Where the Wild Things Are – Maurice Sendak
- Hop on Pop – Dr. Seuss
- The Feminine Mystique – Betty Friedman
- The Cat's Cradle – Kurt Vonnegut
- The Fire Next Time – James Baldwin
- Encyclopedia Brown – Donald J. Sobol
- Why We Can't Wait – Martin Luther King Jr.
- Caravans – James A. Michener
- The Bell Jar – Sylvia Plat

Technological Advancements

Polio Vaccine

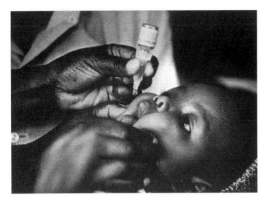

Oral polio vaccine

In 1963, a live OPV (oral vaccine) was introduced and given alongside IPV (injection vaccine) to the main population of both the UK and the US. The OVP proved to be much more successful as it eliminated the need to for sterile injection needles for administration. As a result, during the 1960's the number of people contracting polio in the US went down to fewer than 100 cases and by 1970 fewer than 10. Today, it has nearly been fully eradicated, though it still persists in a handful of countries.

Quasars

Dutch astronomer Maarten Schmidt published the first definitive findings regarding his discovery of quasars in the journal Nature on March 16th, 1963. In his findings, he was able to determine the exact measurement of the distance to a quasar based on the luminescence of the redshift produced by it. It was later determined that the quasars emit such massive amounts of luminosity due to the friction of matter as it is pulled into a black hole. Essentially, the quasar is the part in the nucleus of a galaxy that emits the most luminosity.

Caltech astronomer Maarten Schmidt

The First Liver Transplant

Dr. Thomas E. Starzl, in 1989, as he oversees
a liver transplant

On March 1st, 1963, Thomas Starzl performed the first liver transplant in a human. The recipient, a three-year old child with biliary atresia, did not survive. But in the following decade, several more attempts were made by doctors around the world, all of which were not successful. Technology was changing quickly, however and with the advent of several new scientific breakthroughs, including the advances of immunosuppression with the development of antilymphocyte globulin, an understanding that tissue matching was less important in liver grafting than in kidney transplantation, and improved organ preservation with the use of ex vivo perfusion systems all served to slowly advance the knowledge and practice that has given us all of the capability with regards to liver transplantation and grafting that we have today.

The First Commercial Nuclear Reactor Goes Online

On December 12, 1963, The Jersey Central Power and Light Company purchased a 515-megawatt plant from General Electric to be built at Oyster Creek, New Jersey. It was the first nuclear power purchased

The pressure vessel for the first commercial nuclear power plant in the United States being lowered into place

without government aid and in direct competition with a conventional facility.

AT&T Introduces Touch-Tone Phone

Western Electric 1500 Series touch-tone phone

After three years of testing, AT&T finally introduced the touch-tone telephone, replacing the old dial phones on November 18th, 1963. It had not been possible until the invention of the transistor that the push-button technology became dependable and practical. The following decades touch-tone service was replaced with pulse dialing technology and became the world-wide standard for telecommunication.

The First Prototype Learjet Takes Off

Based on the Swiss-designed single-engine ground-attack FFA P-16 fighter jet, William Powell Lear, Sr. created the Swiss-American Aviation Corporation (SAAC) to produce a two-engine passenger plane: the SAAC-23 Execujet. It was later changed to simply Lear Jet Corp. The first prototype was begun on February

Prototype Learjet 23, N801L, first flight

7th, 1962, and by October 1963, the first prototype was flown. It proceeded to crash due to pilot error when he deployed the wing spoilers while demonstrating an engine failure on takeoff. The Federal Aviation Agency determined that the crash been pilot error and not due to bad design and awarded the Lear Jet 23 its type certificate on July 31st, 1963. By 1966 production of the first model was completed with all one hundred and one orders being fulfilled.

Lava Lamp or The Astro Lamp Launched

The Craven Walkers in the 1960s

Edward Craven Walker invented the lava lamp (or astro lamp) to instant popularity that still endures today. The lava lamp has become synonymous with the quintessential 1960's household adornment (perhaps along with macramé and vinyl records) and was embraced by the hippie movement that came in the later 60's. Walker designed the lamp by using an egg timer and two liquids and it was manufactured initially using cocktail and orange squash bottles. Walker himself was as unique a man as his lamps and is quoted as saying "I think it will always be popular, It's like the cycle of life. It grows, breaks up, falls down and then starts all over again," and 1968, Walker and his wife invited the entire cast for the controversial musical "Hair" to their home in Dorset, England.

Lava lamps of different colors

Fashion

1963 Russ Clothes Ad

The Go-Go Boots

Fashion in 1963 was quite different from previous decades, with various trends and styles in clothing, makeup, and hair. Skirts were typically knee-high, heels were lower, and dresses without sleeves were a popular choice. Leather and fur were all the rage, and women's boots ranged from thigh-high to ankle length.

Paisley patterns were trendy in 1963, as were ascot scarves and textured stockings. Overall, the trend with clothing was comfort with style. Waistlines on women's dresses were no longer cinched but more relaxed and comfortable. The shift dress was popular, and petticoats that were so common in the 1950s had all but disappeared.

Makeup was more subdued as the natural look became more appreciated, and women's hair ranged from the short cropped 'pixie' style to the incredible heights of

(L to R): Brigitte Bardot with a messy beehive; Sleek and timeless Sophia Loren; Nancy Kwan with her famous Vidal Sassoon cut

the 'beehive.' Straightened hair was popular, and this was often created by 'ironing' the hair. This process involved putting a piece of paper or paper bag over the hair to stop it from burning, taking the household iron, and running it over to create straight tresses.

The style in the 1960s was heavily influenced by rock and roll, with the Beatles invasion leading to men copying their style of suits and the mop-top haircut they became world famous for. Until then, most men kept their hair in a short back and sides style, so it was initially considered rebellious for a man to grow his hair long.

Men's flat front no pleat pants

Bold tweeds

Another new trend for men was to have trousers without pleats in the front. Jackets and sweaters were often decorated with stripes, and softer Italian-styled shoes were preferred.

Brighter colors

Color was starting to be incorporated into men's clothing as brighter shades became more popular. Gone were the days of men wearing just blues, greys, and browns. Now they were wearing yellows, reds, and pinks.

For both men and women, fur trim on coats and jackets was the trend, and turtlenecks with vests were starting to make an appearance.

For professional women, their style was heavily influenced by Jackie Kennedy, wife of President John F Kennedy, with her matching two-piece suits with oversized buttons and pillbox hats. Capes and coats were also commonly sought after, and women wore trousers and bellbottoms a lot more than they had in the past. Gloves were still worn from time to time, but mainly for special occasions, not their daily usage in the 1950s.

Jackie Kennedy outfit styles

Cars of 1963

1963 was a stellar year for car manufacturers, with total sales of passenger cars being 7,636, 993. It was the second largest in US history, behind 1955.

🏆 Top selling car of 1963

1963 Buick Riviera

The top selling car of the year was the Buick Riviera. 1963 was Buick's first unique Riviera model and a total of 1,127,261 Rivieras were produced. The Riviera was initially a front engine/rear-wheel drive platform, but switched to front-wheel drive starting with the 1979 model. The name Riviera, Latin for "coastline", was meant to evoke the allure and affluence of the French Riviera.

🚗 Sports cars of 1963

Aston Martin DB5

1963 Aston Martin DB5

The Aston Martin DB5 is considered to be perhaps the most beautiful Aston Martin ever produced, particularly the specially equipped silver birch DB5 that starred in the James Bond films Goldfinger and Thunderball, which made the DB5 famous. It was very similar in make to the DB4 with a few improvements: The V6 engine increased its capacity to 4 liters by increasing the bore to 96mm, the introduction of a true full synchromesh ZF 5 speed gearbox, and the adoption of the Girling disc brakes that had only been used on the DB4GT, and 15" wheels. A convertible version was also offered.

Shelby Cobra 289

The 163 Shelby Cobra was the first largely successful English-American hybrid. It combined the power of Ford's short-stroke V8 with the nimbleness of AC's racing capabilities. The idea was motivated by racing legend Carol Shelby, who raced and

1963 Shelby Cobra 289

refined the vehicle with Ford's funds. AC Cars modified their Ace chassis to accept Ford's V8 engine and shipped bare chassis to Shelby American where they were fitted for Ford's 260 cu in. engine. The engine worked so well in the spacious engine bay that Shelby moved to the 289 unit in 1964. The development was relatively simple, and the Cobra started winning races from the first. It had a tremendously good power to weight ratio that bettered with both the 289 and 427 engines. In short order, the Cobra accumulated an impressive racing record and won the GT Championship in 1964 and placed fourth at Le Mans the same year.

Chevrolet Corvette "Stingray" split window

The Corvette "Stingray" got its shape and styling from the shortfin mako shark, of which a photo hung in miniature in the head of GM Design, Bill Mitchell's office. In 1963, the distinction between road and race cars was growing. The Sting Ray's body style, beautiful as it may be, proved to be

1963 Chevrolet Corvette Stingray

difficult for the racing department of GM and adjustments had to be made before it could hit the track. It did alright – that is, until the Cobra came along and begun to win everything. But as a road car, the Sting Ray was an overwhelming success.

Alpine A110

The Alpine A110 began its journey to success with sports-bodied Renaults, and soon led to complete car construction. The A110, like its A106 predecessor, featured a steel tube backbone chassis and fiberglass bodywork.

Its rear mounted engine Renault Inline-4 was upgraded each year. Starting with a 998cc unit, the car moved from 77bhp to 155 bhp by 1970. The final version of the A110 was the 1970 1600S. It won the 1971 Monte Carlo Rally and the European Championship of 1970.

1963 Alpine A110

Austin-Healey 3000 MKIII BJ8

1963 Austin-Healey 3000 MKIII BJ8

The "Big Healey", or the BJ8 as it was nicknamed, was the final and most sophisticated of Austin-Healy. It boasted a new 150 bhp engine and a more luxurious interior, with numerous detail differences around the car. Road & Track were quoted as saying the BJ8 was "an enthusiast's sports car that was fun to drive with lots of performance and good handling and braking characteristics."

🚗 Road Cars of 1963

Chevvy Suburban

By 1963, the iconic surf-mobile was already in its fifth generation. In 1963, it made waves by offering 4x4 for the very first time and its popularity was only enhanced.

1963 Chevy Suburban

With seating for up to 8 passengers, it was the perfect family vehicle, and some were even modified to fit up to 15 people! Classic car market range: $13,400 to $64,800.

Jeep Wagoneer

The 1963 Jeep Wagoneer was another fabulous choice in the budget-friendly luxury market. It made its debut in 1963 and is considered to be the first American SUV. It offered comfort, with independent suspension, automatic windows, a radio, heater, and even had off-road capacities. Classic car market range: $6,000 to $66,000

1963 Jeep Wagoneer

Chevy Impala

1963 Chevrolet Impala

The classic low-rider enthusiasts' car today, in 1963 it was a high-end family car, built with tall, wide, and low body to provide comfort for a family of five, or in the case of a family of nine for anyone who opted for the Impala wagon. The interior came with leather-like, soft, vinyl upholstery and aluminum trim and set the bar for family car comfort. Classic car market range: $9,075 to $54,500

Chevy C/K 10

1963 Chevy C/K 10

A coil-spring front suspension was introduced on the Chevy C/K 10 pickup in 1963 and transformed this utility truck into a comfortable ride. Though simple in its display and features, but it remained popular because it was a reliable working truck. Its long bench seat in the cab was spacious and could easily accommodate 3 people. Easy to modify and customize, many can be found on the classic car show circuit today, but you might still see a few being put to use on the farm still in 2022. Classic car market range: $20,200 to $95,400

Jaguar S-type

The Jaguar S-type is a British-made saloon car produced from 1963 to 1968. It was a more luxurious alternative to the Mark 2, without the large size of the Mark X. When the S-type was released in 1963. The Mark 2 still remained unexpectedly strong in

1963 Jaguar S-type

sales, despite its age, and though introduced in 1963, only a small number of S-Types was produced in that year, producing only 43.

Popular Recreation

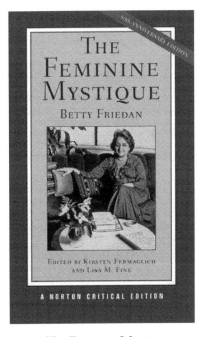

The Feminine Mystique

One of the most popular books in 1963 was 'The Feminine Mystique' written by Betty Friedan, and it is acknowledged that it helped establish the Feminist Movement. It sold more than 1 million copies and challenged the previously accepted idea that women should only be housewives and mothers.

Regarding toys, some of the most popular were Mouse Trap, the Easy-Bake Oven, and Big Loo. The Big Loo was a robot toy that stood at the height of three feet, or 37 inches, and was made with particular polystyrene parts. The eyes flashed red, and the hand-cranked voice box had ten different messages recorded. Darts could be fired from the back of the robot using triggers, and balls could be fired from the hands. It was able to squirt water from the belly button and had a Morse code clicker, a compass, a bell, and a whistle.

Mouse trap was a board game for up to four players and was one of the first three-dimensional board games to be mass-produced. Also popular were the Troll Dolls, originally called 'Dam Things.' It was a plastic doll with up-combed brightly colored hair,

1963 'Mouse Trap' Board Game

75

The first three versions of 'Easy-Bake Oven'

created by Thomas Dam, a Danish woodcutter. They were one of the biggest toy fads in the US from 1963 to 1965 and have had a recent resurgence in popularity, with the dolls being manufactured again and movies and merchandise hitting the market in the last few years. The Easy-Bake Oven is still being produced today but was introduced to the consumer market in 1963. It was heated by two light bulbs and came with little round cooking pans and packets of cake mix, which could also be purchased separately. In its first year, 500,000 were sold.

Rock and roll and pop music traversed from vinyl records at home to live concerts in 1963. More bands were performing live, and it was common to see young women swooning at the likes of Elvis Presley and the Beatles in the audience. Go-go dancing was popular, and the television show 'American Bandstand' became a staple fixture for teens particularly each week.

Barbie and G.I. Joe were popular, as were slot cars and yo-yos. Card games were a favorite pastime, particularly with adults, who would get together and play bridge, euchre, or poker. One of the most popular activities for all people, young and old, was indoor bowling. The influence of

Early versions of Barbie and G.I. Joe

the Kennedy Administration led to touch football and sailing being popular activities. Surfing was a great trending activity, and skateboarding was becoming more popular.

1963 Leica M3

One of the most popular hobbies in 1963 was photography. Cameras were a lot easier to use, and the flashbulbs were built in, which made the camera easier to carry around and get snapshots of daily life. Cartridge film was also available, so it was easy to take the photos and drop off the film roll to get it developed. With these advancements, anyone could own and use a camera, and photo albums could be filled with black and white photographs of memories.

Chapter VI: Births & Deaths 1963

Births (onthisday.com)

Rand Paul - January 7th - American politician

Hakeem Olajuwon - January 21st - Nigerian basketball player

José Mourinho - January 26th - Portuguese football manager

Michael Jordan - February 17th - American Basketball player

Charles Barkley - February 20th - American Basketball player

Vanessa Williams - March 18th - American singer

David Thewlis - March 20th - British actor

Quentin Tarantino - March 27th - American film director

Julian Lennon - April 8th - Musician/son of John Lennon

Conan O'Brien - April 18th - American comedian

Jet Li - April 26th - Chinese actor/martial artist

Natasha Richardson - May 11th - British actress

Mike Myers - May 25th - American Actor

Jason Isaacs - June 6th - British actor

Johnny Depp - June 9th - American actor

Helen Hunt - June 15th - American actress

Laura Ingraham - June 19th - American conservative television host/ Fox News television host

George Michael - June 25th - American musician

Edie Falco – July 5th - American actress

Mikael Pernfors – July 16th – Swedish Tennis Player

Lisa Kudrow - July 30th - American actress

Norman Cook (Fatboy Slim) – July 31st - British musician and record producer

Coolio - Aug 1st - American rapper

Mark Strong - August 5th - British actor

Whitney Houston - August 9th - American singer

John Stamos - August 19th - American actor

Hideo Kojima - August 24th – Japanese Game designer

Randy Johnson – September 10th – American Baseball player

Theodoros Roussopoulos – September 13th - Greek politician

Elisabeth Shue - October 6th - American actress

Rob Schneider - October 31st - American actor/ screenwriter

Big Kenny - November 1st - American country singer

Tatum O'Neal - November 5th - American actress

Brad Pitt - December 18th - American actor

Mike Pompeo – December 30th – American politician

Scott Ian – December 31st - American heavy metal guitarist

Deaths (onthisday.com)

Dick Powell - January 2nd - American actor/musician/ director/producer

Jack Carson - January 2nd – Canadian-born, American actor

Rogers Hornsby - January 5th - American baseball player/coach

Robert Frost - January 29th - American poet

Patsy Cline - March 5th - American country singer

Hal Le Sueur - May 3rd - American actor

Pope John XXIII - June 3rd - Pope

ZaSu Pitts - June 7th - American actress

Pedro Armendáriz - June 18th - Mexican actor

Gordon Jones - June 20th - American actor

Patrick Bouvier Kennedy - August 9th - Infant son of JFK

W. E. B. Du Bois - August 27th - American sociologist/civil rights activist/historian

Édith Piaf - October 10th - French singer

Jean Cocteau - October 11th - French poet/playwright/ novelist/designer/filmmaker/ visual artist

Douglas Croft - October 24th - American actor/ soldier

Adolphe Menjou - October 29th - American actor

Henry Daniell - October 31st - English actor

C. S. Lewis - November 22nd - British author

Aldous Huxley - November 22nd - English writer/ philosopher

John F. Kennedy - November 22nd - President of the United States

Karyn Kupcinet - November 28th - American actress

Sabu - December 2nd - Indian actor

 Barbara Read - December 12th – Canadian-American actress

 Yasujiro Ozu - December 12th - Japanese film director/screenwriter

 Dinah Washington - December 14th - American singer

Chapter VII: Statistics 1963

* US GDP 1963 - 1.67 trillion US $ (worldbank.org)

* US GDP 2021 - 96.1 trillion US $ (worldbank.org)

* UK GDP 1963 - 86.56 billion US $ (worldbank.org)

* UK GDP 2021 - 3.19 trillion US $ (worldbank.org)

* U.S. Inflation (% Change in C.P.I.) 1963 (worldbank.org) - 1.2%

* US Inflation - (% Change in C.P.I.) 2022 (worldbank.org) - 4.7%

* UK. Inflation (% Change in C.P.I.) 1963 (worldbank.org) - 2%

* UK Inflation (% Change in C.P.I.) 2022 (worldbank.org) - 2.5%

* U.S. Population by Gender 1963 - F: 95,575,715 M: 93,666,285 (worldbank.org)

* U.S. Population by Gender 2021 - F: 167,669,677 M: 164,224,068 (worldbank.org)

* UK. Population by Gender 1963 - F: 27,667,276 M: 25,982,724 (worldbank.org)

* UK. Population by Gender 2021 - F: 34,045,551 M: 33,281,018 (worldbank.org)

* U.S. Life Expectancy at Birth 1963 - 70 (worldbank.org)

* U.S. Life Expectancy at Birth 2021 - 77 (worldbank.org)

* U.K. Life Expectancy at Birth 1963 - 71 (worldbank.org)

* U.K. Life Expectancy at Birth 2020 - 81 (worldbank.org)

* U.S. Annual Working Hours Per Worker 1963 - 1,927 (ourworldindata.org)

* U.S. Annual Working Hours Per Worker 2017 - 1,757 (ourworldindata.org)

* U.K. Annual Working Hours Per Worker 1963 - 2,021 (ourworldindata.org)

* U.K. Annual Working Hours Per Worker 2017 - 1,670 (ourworldindata.org)

* U.S. Unemployment Rate 1963 - 5.5% (thebalancemoney.com)

* U.S. Unemployment Rate 2021 - 3.9%(thebalancemoney.com)

* U.K. Unemployment Rate 1963- 4.9% (bls.gov)

* U.K. Unemployment Rate 2022 - 3.8% (ons.gov.uk)

* U.S. Total Tax Revenue 1963 - 107 billion USD (thebalancemoney.com)

* U.S. Total Tax Revenue 2022 - 2.6 trillion USD (businessinsider.com)

* U.K. Total Tax Revenue 1963 - 6.29 billion (ukpublicrevenue.co.uk)

* U.K. Total Tax Revenue 2022 - 178.4 billion (gov.uk)

* U.S. Prison Population 1963 - 350,000 (prisonstudies.org)

* U.S. Prison Population 2022 - 2.1 million (prisonstudies.org)

* U.K. Prison Population 1963 - 30,000 (prisonstudies.org)

* U.K. Prison Population 2020 - 12,747 (prisonstudies.org)

* ✷ U.S. Cost of Living: $100 in 1963 has the same "purchasing power" or "buying power" as $968.34 in 2022. That is a total change of 8.68% in sixty years (in2013dollars.com).

* ✷ U.K. Cost of Living: £100 in 1963 would equate to the spending power of £3,327.51 in 2022. That is a total change of 2,228% in sixty years (in2013dollars.com).

* ✷ Average cost of new house 1963 US - 18,000 USD (gobankingrates.com)

* ✷ Average Cost of new house US 2022 - 348,000 USD (gobankingrates.com)

* ✷ Average cost of new house 1963 UK - 2,840 British pounds (gobankingrates.com)

* ✷ Average Cost of new house 2022 UK - 281,000 British pounds (gobankingrates.com)

* ✷ Average income per year 1963 US - 6,200 USD (worldpopulationreview.com)

* ✷ Average income per year 2022 US - 106,000 USD (worldpopulationreview.com)

* ✷ Average income per year 2022 UK - 4,396.64 British pounds (ukpublicrevenue.co.uk)

* ✷ Average income per year 2022 UK - 31,447 British pounds (ukpublicrevenue.co.uk)

Cost Of Things

In 1963, the cost of various things, be it a house or a loaf of bread, was considerably different to what people would pay in 2023. Here are some of the prices charged for various items in 1963:

United States

* ✷ Fresh eggs (1 dozen): $0.55 (stacker.com)
* ✷ White bread (1 pound): $0.22 (stacker.com)
* ✷ Sliced bacon (1 pound): $0.68 (stacker.com)
* ✷ Round steak (1 pound): $1.06 (stacker.com)
* ✷ Potatoes (10 pounds): $0.65 (stacker.com)
* ✷ Fresh delivered milk (1/2 gallon): $0.52 (stacker.com)
* ✷ Coke (.33 L): $0.05 (aag.com)
* ✷ Gas per Gallon: - $0.32 (aag.com)
* ✷ Pack of cigarettes: $0.35 (aag.com)
* ✷ Box of Cheerios: $0.26 (aag.com)
* ✷ Average cost of a new car: $3,233.00 (aag.com)
* ✷ Concert ticket: $5.50 (aag.com)

United Kingdom

* ✷ Gallon of Petrol: 5 shillings (silversurfers.com)
* ✷ Pint of Beer: 2 shillings (retrowow.co.uk)
* ✷ Pack of cigarettes: 4 shillings (retrowow.co.uk)
* ✷ Ford Cortina car: £675 (silversurfers.com)
* ✷ Pepsi Cola (3 cans): 2 shillings (retrowow.co.uk)

* Frigidaire SheerLook refrigerator: £39 (retrowow.co.uk)

* Hoover Constellation 862 vacuum cleaner: £19 and 12 shillings (retrowow.co.uk)

* Kodak Automatic cine camera: £24 and 10 shillings (retrowow.co.uk)

* Rolls-Colston Mk IV dishwasher: £78 and 15 shillings (retrowow.co.uk)

* 112 pounds of coal delivered: 8 to 12 shillings (retrowow.co.uk)

Chapter VIII: Iconic Advertisements of 1963

Chrysler

Martini & Rossi

Arnott's Biscuits

Coca-Cola

Kent

Hunt

Bell Telephone System

Johnnie Walker Red Label

Philips

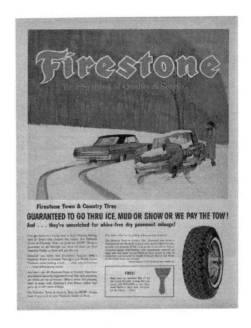

Firestone

Lavazza

Volkswagen

Pepsi-Cola

Booth's Gin

Chesterfield King

Kellogg's Corn Flakes

Kodak Retina 35 mm Camera

7 Up

Plymouth

Budweiser

Royal

Campbell's Soup

IBM

Jose Cuervo Tequila

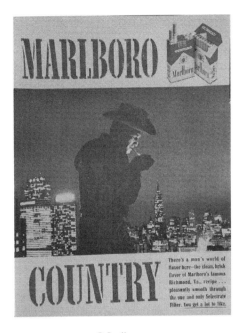

Marlboro   Coca-Cola

I have a gift for you!

Dear reader, thank you so much for reading my book!

To make this book more (much more!) affordable, the images are all black & white, but I've created a special gift for you!

You can now have access, for FREE, to the PDF version of this book with the original images!

Keep in mind that some are originally black & white, but a lot of them are colored.

I hope you enjoy it!

Download it here:

http://bit.ly/3uoeAGm

Or Scan this QR Code:

I have a favor to ask you!

I deeply hope you've enjoyed reading this book and felt transported right into 1963!

I loved researching it, organizing it, and writing it, knowing that it would make your day a little brighter.

If you've enjoyed it too, I would be extremely grateful if you took just a few minutes to leave a positive customer review and share it with your friends.

As an unknown author, that makes all the difference and gives me the extra energy I need to keep researching, writing, and bringing joy to all my readers. Thank you!

Best regards,
Richard J. Thomas

Please leave a positive book review here:

http://bit.ly/3XOPPR4

Or Scan this QR Code:

Check Our Other Books!

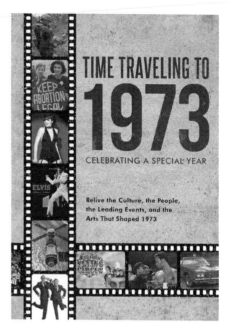

Made in United States
Troutdale, OR
05/27/2023